FIRST BIOGRAPHIES

Harriet Tubman

Cassie Mayer

Heinemann Library
Chicago, Illinois

© 2008 Heinemann Library
a division of Reed Elsevier Inc.
Chicago, Illinois

Customer Service **888-454-2279**

Visit our Web site at **www.heinemannlibrary.com**

Photo research by Tracy Cummins
Designed by Kimberly R. Miracle
Maps by Mapping Specialists, Ltd.
Printed and bound in China by South China Printing Company

10 09 08 07
10 9 8 7 6 5 4 3 2 1

10 Digit ISBN: 1-4034-9973-X (hc)   1-4034-9982-9 (pb)

Library of Congress Cataloging-in-Publication Data
Mayer, Cassie.
  Harriet Tubman / Cassie Mayer.
     p. cm. -- (First biographies)
  Includes bibliographical references and index.
  ISBN-13: 978-1-4034-9973-8 (hc)
  ISBN-13: 978-1-4034-9982-0 (pb)
  1. Tubman, Harriet, 1820?-1913--Juvenile literature. 2. Slaves--United States--Biography--Juvenile literature. 3. Women slaves--United States--Biography--Juvenile literature. 4. African American women--Biography--Juvenile literature. 5. African Americans--Biography--Juvenile literature. 6. Underground Railroad--Juvenile literature. I. Title.
  E444.T82M366 2008
  973.7'115092--dc22
  [B]
                          2007009992

Acknowledgements
The author and publisher are grateful to the following for permission to reproduce copyright material: ©The Art Archive **pp. 11** (Culver Pictures), **14** (Culver Pictures); ©The Bridgeman Art Library **pp. 12** (Private Collection), **23** (Private Collection); ©Corbis **pp. 4, 5** (Bettmann), **8** (Bettmann), **18** (Bettmann); ©Darlene Bordwell **pp. 21, 23**; ©Getty Images **pp. 16** (MPI), **19** (MPI), **23** (MPI); ©The Granger Collection **p. 17**; ©Harcourt Education **pp. 7** (Sean Victory), **10** (Sean Victory); ©Library of Congress Prints and Photographs Division **pp. 15, 22**; ©Lonely Planet Images **p. 20** (Kim Grant); ©North Wind Pictures Archives **pp. 6, 9**.

Cover image reproduced with permission of the ©Library of Congress Prints and Photographs Division. Back cover image reproduced with permission of ©Harcourt Education (Sean Victory).

Contents

Introduction

Harriet Tubman was a leader.
A leader helps change things.

Tubman helped free slaves. Slaves were people owned by other people.

Early Life

Tubman was born around 1820.
She lived in Maryland.

She was a slave.

Slavery

Slaves could not choose how they lived.

Most slaves were black.

Escape

Tubman escaped slavery in 1849.

She was helped by other people.
The people were part of a special group.

The Underground Railroad

The group was called the Underground Railroad. The group helped slaves escape.

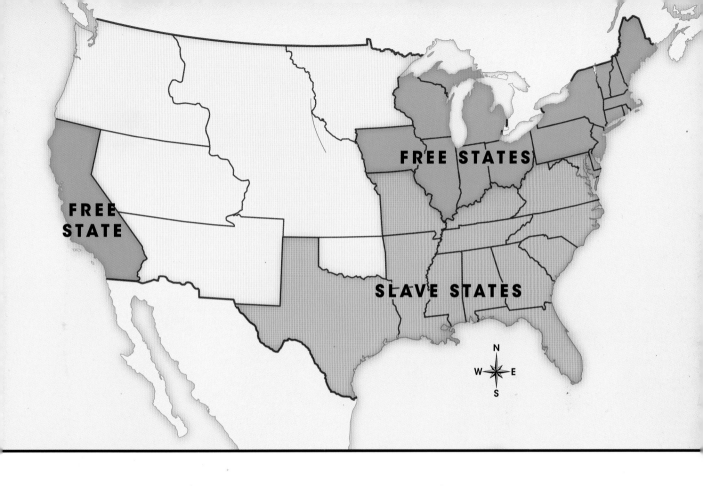

FREE STATES

FREE STATE

SLAVE STATES

The group helped them reach the northern states. Northern states did not have slavery.

Tubman became a leader of the
Underground Railroad.

She was very smart.
She helped many slaves escape.

Civil War

The southern states fought the northern states in 1861. This was called the Civil War.

The northern states won the Civil War in 1865. Slaves became free.

Some people still did not treat black people well. Some people did not think they were equal.

Tubman believed all people were equal.

Tubman always spoke about her beliefs.

Tubman died in 1913.
She was given a special funeral.

Why We Remember Her

Harriet Tubman was a brave leader.
She helped many people become free.

Picture Glossary

Civil War a war in the United States. People in the northern states and southern states fought each other.

Underground Railroad a group of people that secretly helped slaves escape.

Timeline

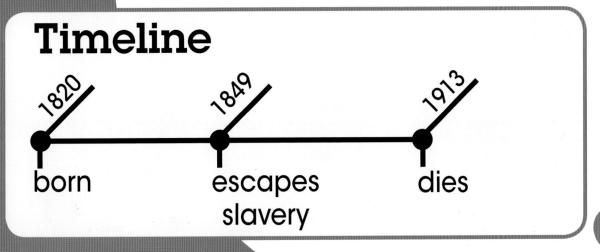

1820 — born

1849 — escapes slavery

1913 — dies

Index

Note to Parents and Teachers

This series introduces prominent historical figures, focusing on the significant events of each person's life and their impact on American society. Illustrations and primary sources are used to enhance students' understanding of the text.

The text has been carefully chosen with the advice of a literacy expert to enable beginning readers success while reading independently or with moderate support. An expert in the field of early childhood social studies curriculum was consulted to provide interesting and appropriate content.

You can support children's nonfiction literacy skills by helping students use the table of contents, headings, picture glossary, and index.